How To Preach

William Booth

Compilation and Comments
by
Charles Talmadge

THE SALVATION ARMY
New York, New York

HOW TO PREACH

Part I reprinted from a series of articles entitled "How to Preach," written by William Booth and appearing in *The Officer* magazine from May through August, 1893.

Copyright © 1979 by The Salvation Army
Eastern Territory Literary Council
145 West 15th Street
New York, N.Y. 10011

ISBN 0-89216-026-8

Printed in the United States of America

CONTENTS

Section Two

PREFACE

WILLIAM Booth, Founder of the Salvation Army and one of the great preachers of his day, reached thousands with the gospel. His son, Bramwell Booth, wrote in *Echoes and Memories* — "Thanks to the advantage of the railway and the steamship and in his later years the motor car, the voice of William Booth was heard by greater multitudes of every race and nation than the voice of any mortal man had been heard before."

His preaching was effective and brought conviction to the hearts of listeners; decisions for Christ by those who came to hear him were counted in the thousands.

In 1904 the author Harold Begbie accompanied William Booth for the first few days of a motor tour that was to span England. Mr. Begbie published his impression of the General's manner of preaching in an article that appeared in the August 12th London *Daily Mail* for that year. "One discovers the longer one listens to General Booth, a nobleness of diction in his oratory. It is all simple and rugged and real. The general result is the conviction of the eternal and infinite mysteries, and the uplifting and magnifying of the spiritual existence in each separate soul before him."

After a meeting held at Congress Hall in London, England, an incident occurred that provides an illustration of the Founder's earnest desire to reach the souls of all men with the Lord's message.

It had been a great night at the Congress Hall, the old tiered hall had been packed almost to the ceiling. There had been great music and great singing, and at the last, hundreds seeking Christ at the penitent-form.

At the close of the meeting, the Founder, exhausted, was taken to "The General's Room" where he rested and drank warm milk.

The young officer "on the door" seeing the old man alone and obviously tired, felt he should do something to cheer the Founder up. So he stepped in, and enthusiastically spoke of the meeting, "The crowds ... how they listened ... and the singing ... and General, how wonderful to see that long procession to the Mercy Seat ..."

The Founder looked at the youth for a moment, then shook his head. "Yes, yes, it was a good meeting ... but did you see that other procession? Those who were going out of the hall, out into the night, without Christ?"

Yes, this was the man—a man on fire for the souls of men. A man on fire for his Lord and Saviour, Jesus Christ.

The methods William Booth used and the plan he followed, not only in the preparation of sermons but in the actual preaching, are still valid and fortunately are available for reexamination. To inform the officers of his day, the Founder wrote a series of articles on the subject "How to Preach." They were published during 1893 in the following issues of *The Officer* magazine: May (Vol. 1, No. 5), June (Vol. 1, No. 6), July (Vol. 1, No. 7) and August (Vol. 1, No. 8).

For convenience and clarity these articles have been rearranged in Section I under four chapter headings, but the material is basically the same as it appeared in *The Officer.*

Secton II of this updated presentation has been divided into three parts.

Part One is a summary of the main ideas contained in the articles for *The Officer* using the Founder's own words. It reiterates the plan and methods followed by this great preacher of yesteryear.

Part Two consists of excerpts from sermons of William Booth. These words are from some of the Founder's great sermons which God was pleased to use to His honor and glory.

The quotations from contemporary writers found in *Part Three* convey the tremendous impression William Booth made upon those who witnessed him preach. These firsthand observations confirm that the Founder understood the needs and means for effective preaching; they substantiate and support the methods he pronounced originally in *The Officer* magazine.

The gospel was preached before it was written. So long as hearts are human and so long as tongues know how to speak, the hungry heart will listen to a person who has learned the story of Jesus and His love. The Founder proved this again and again.

The Salvation Army and the Church today need great preachers of the Word. Every officer stands in the line of great succession. Giants such as William Booth, Samuel Logan Brengle, Evangeline Booth, Albert Orsborn, Clarence Wiseman have preceded us. It is hoped that many will profit by all that is said here and will honestly endeavor to follow in the footsteps of the Founder as preachers whom God is pleased to use.

When you stand behind the sacred desk remember you are to make people feel the presence of God and their responsibility to Him! Read carefully all that William Booth suggests and better preaching will be the result.

. . . *Charles Talmadge*

William Booth—the Preacher

— Christine E. McMillan

IT is now 65 years since the Founder was promoted to Glory, and few now living, have adult memories of this man whose burning passion was "Christ for the world—the world for Christ." Like a nova, he rose, burned with a living flame and died, and there has been none like him to this day.

The Founder was among those who are remembered as larger than life. These were of their day, served that day and left the stage. They left no heirs to their greatness. Their names live not only in their recorded deeds and stone memorials, but in the immortal memory of man. Such a one was William Booth.

He came from "respectable" poverty. As a young man he worked in a pawn shop in his native city of Nottingham, making firsthand observations of the course of the decline and fall of the British workman through lack of work, poverty and drink. First the clothes were "popped" (pawned) on Monday morning to be taken out on Saturday to preserve a decent "Sunday front;" then household goods were taken in, to remain; and finally the workman's tools, the last step on the road to total destitution and perhaps the point of no return.

Called to preach the gospel and sure of his vocation William came to London, to become appalled by the depths of misery, poverty, the abandonment to drink and to vice of all kinds, by the denizens of London's East End.

A pragmatic visionary, Booth combined the most farseeing, comprehensive scheme of social welfare to appear since the First Elizabeth, together with a bold and daring venture out into the teeming streets, bearing the pure and simple gospel of the love of God and His power to redeem the human soul and life. The people listened. They came by the thousands to "converted" saloons and disreputable theaters, to kneel at the feet of Christ and enter into newness of life.

We are familiar with his picture—the large nose, the flowing beard—but what did he really look like as he faced those great audiences, to preach, "as a dying man to dying men?"

Commissioner Yamamuro said, on the occasion of the Founder's first visit to Japan: " . . . we saw before us his erect and military figure and the poise of his beautiful head, crowned with its snow-white hair . . . "

But it is left to William Booth's son Bramwell, in his book *Echoes and Memories,* to give a vivid picture of the Founder in Action:

> His voice was powerful without being loud. He could by an effort, compass an immense area and hold a great throng spellbound.
>
> His opening was customarily quiet, almost lamb-like. It was an astonishing contrast— his striking and aggressive appearance and the gentleness with which he began to talk. No loud, sensational beginning could have arrested an audience so completely. Warming

to his topic he would introduce incidents by way of illustration or appeal out of his own experience, going on to a final appeal sparing nothing in directness, urged with tremendous energy in which the whole man, body, soul and spirit seemed to share.

Sometimes even at moments of great tension, his manner would be very subdued, and I liked him best then. At other times action would accompany almost every sentence. Head, arms, hands, feet—the whole frame would vibrate and tremble as the subject or the audience or both, stirred him.

His sensationalism cannot be denied. He adopted it when it seemed to be the best lever wherewith to pry open the insensitive mind. The aim of his sensationalism was to startle and shock the people whom an ordinary appeal about their danger or the evil of their sins would leave unmoved.

He would picture Lot going out to warn his sons-in-law on the last night in Sodom. He would turn up his coat collar and seize any hat which happened to be at hand, to suggest a man going out on an imperious, though disagreeable errand. The whole congregation would be given the feeling of the dark night, the knocking at the door, the coming doom, and then the hollow laughter of the young men.

Again it might be a representation of the

various classes of sinners suffering their doom in the regions of the lost, and among them, one, counting something, always counting, counting. The audience would hold its breath while he himself counted: "One—two—three —four—five." I have seen thousands of people transfixed as the counting proceeded—"ten— eleven—twelve—thirteen." Then "twenty-eight —twenty-nine—THIRTY!" Why it's Judas!

How many actors could hold an immense audience spellbound while merely counting to thirty?

In *Echoes and Memories* Bramwell Booth recalls the Founder's intense personal commitment to his vocation, his attitude about himself and his chosen life's work.

> One of the greatest talkers of his age, my father was yet most diffident about his own powers. Many a time in great auditoriums he has said to me just before rising to speak, "Pray for me; I feel like sinking through the floor." He has again and again declared himself unequal to the occasion and the opportunity.

> He rarely allowed himself to use notes in his great meetings. He preached often when he was little prepared, sometimes when he was not prepared at all; often again under the compulsion of haste, or in fatigue even to the point of exhaustion. Yet after he had arisen . . . the depression was as a rule soon

shaken off, his frailty seemed to disappear, and presently he suggested nothing so much as a fighting champion triumphing in the fray.

His gestures were at times deliberately illustrative, and not due merely to the vehemence of his utterance. Once in a railway carriage he said to one of his officers, "My arms are not long enough to reach both rich and poor. When I am in touch with the poor"—bringing one hand toward the floor— "I am out of touch with the rich"—and the other hand went toward the roof, "And when I am in touch with the rich—I lose touch with the poor." And then, letting both hands drop, he said, as if thinking aloud, "I very much doubt whether God Almighty's arms are long enough." This was very much his platform method too.

However, all his attention-getting devices were directed toward the simple goal of making the message clear and plain. To quote Bramwell Booth once again, "He was a messenger to the heart of mankind. His appeal was to the conscience. He believed that to every soul there was a judgment seat, continually approving or condemning. It was to that tribunal he appealed."

No meeting or preaching engagement ever became routine to William Booth. In that hour, or two hours, decisons would be made for life or for death. No moment nor word must be wasted lest a dying soul might be forever lost.

I recall a particular story concerning the Founder

fondly recounted by my mother, Mrs. Commissioner John McMillan. It is a story that illustrates the impact William Booth's words had on the lives of those who came to hear him speak, and conveys his deep commitment to "go for the souls" of all men—especially those he felt most in need of grace.

Near the close of the 19th century the Sydney, Australia, Town Hall, all white and crimson and gold, was packed to the farthest gallery for the three great meetings addressed by the Founder. On the platform were representatives of government, the churches, politics, as well as the aristocracy of Sydney society.

Among the throng was a young woman who had come up from the country to see and hear William Booth. She had become interested in The Salvation Army, although a devout Anglican and member of the Church of England. She had come to a crossroads as she debated the course her life should take.

The singular opportunity of going to medical school had been offered to her. She could become a teacher, or a deaconess of her own church. On the other hand, perhaps this day would resolve her indecisions.

She was enthralled by the great gatherings and deeply moved, but the guidance she had sought did not seem to be forthcoming as she prepared to return home at the close of the night meeting. On the way out, she discovered that there was to be another meeting, held in the Salvation Army hall, at midnight.

She couldn't imagine what it could be but having made up her mind to miss nothing, she let her train go, and at midnight came to the hall to discover that it was full and she was shut out. However, she had made up her mind, so by pleading and threatening, she was at last allowed in and was seated on the stairs leading up to the platform.

And what a sight! Here gathered in the hundreds were the offscouring of the Sydney streets—prostitutes, drunks, opium sellers and users, in all their misery and lostness. And speaking to them was not the great leader of a world Army, a general of a great fighting force, but rather a tender father, a lover who opened his heart in compassion and love, to woo them back into the world of light and life.

My mother came away to make the decision of her life, to choose the Cross as the way of Light.

Long after that she learned the reason for the midnight meeting. At the close of the last meeting in the Town Hall, as they were all congratulating the old man on the success of the day, he turned upon them saying, "Those are not the people I came thousands of miles to reach. Where were the drunkards and the prostitutes? Where were the lost sheep?" And exhausted as he must have been, he came to those to whom he had given his heart and his soul and his life, long ago, in London's East End.

Attend the closing words of an address to officers. The language is different from ours today, but we are moved strangely by the passion of this God-blessed man.

If the same burning motivation moves the spirit, and the soul longs to bring all men everywhere into the light and joy and victory of the Everlasting Gospel, the words will be given, and the shining bounds of the Kingdom extended.

On to Calvary! On to death for the world! Let us not refuse the smiters! No halting! No rest! On, suffering, sorrowing, weeping, dying for God and men, till the hosts of hell fly from their last defense, and we march on over a burning world into everlasting glory!

Section One

(The actual words of William Booth,
with minimal editing)

Let us make earth as much like Heaven as we can, by multiplying the number of loving hearts in it, whose chief care is not to protect their own rights and make others minister to their welfare, but who partake of the spirit of the Master, who came not to be ministered unto, but to minister, and left us the commandment that we should love one another even as He loved us.

. . . William Booth

CHAPTER I

The Sacredness of our Responsibility

I WANT to have a quiet talk with my officers on the subject of preaching viewed from a Salvation Army standpoint. You will know that by preaching I mean that kind of talking which is calculated to make men understand and seek salvation—nay, which will help them to find it and spread it abroad.

I have always felt a difficulty in speaking about this subject, and when I have tried to do so in officers' meetings I have seldom succeeded to my satisfaction. In attempting the task now I need not say that nothing is further from my intention than to make any officers formal—than the setting forth of any plan likely to encourage anything like formal sermonizing. I desire just the opposite, and although very doubtful as to how I shall succeed, I will make an effort, trusting in the Spirit of God to guide me in what I am about to say.

Personal Experience

One of the first things absolutely essential to effective preaching is the personal realization on the part of the speaker of the things preached about. He must know in his own soul that the things he proclaims to others are what he declares them to be. There can be no effective preaching of salvation without the actual personal experience of the things spoken of in the heart and mind of the speaker. How can a man intelligently and effectively describe the evil of sin who has not had his eyes opened by the Holy Spirit to see something of it in his own soul? How can a man describe conversion who has not himself gone through the change? It is so all through the range of salvation experience.

Personal Testimony

The apostle John says: *"That which was from the beginning, which we have heard, which we have seen with our eyes, which we have looked upon, and our hands have handled of the Word of Life, declare we unto you, that ye also may have fellowship with us"* (1 John 1:1,2). That is, we apostles know from our own personal contact with Jesus Christ and our own experience of His love, that His salvation is a good and blessed reality, and therefore with confidence proclaim Him to you, and press it upon your acceptance.

Here is the secret of the great power of testimony—especially in the case of new converts who know nothing about theology and the forms and ceremonies of religion, who can do nothing more than tell the wonderful things He has actually done for them. Mere theorizing about religion has very little power—is all but useless, however clearly and cleverly it may be expressed without the combination with it of testimony.

Audiences will go to sleep under the most eloquent disquisition about religion. Explanations of the simplest character and appeals all on fire with human energy will fall powerless, where the plain statements of deliverance from sin and fear and hell, and of the realization of love and peace and power in the soul, will create feeling and bring proud, stubborn men and women to the mercy-seat.

It follows, therefore, that for an officer to speak effectively of the things of God he must be soundly converted, and either have experienced the blessing of perfect love or be on full stretch to find it, and have been baptized after a Pentecostal fashion with an all-consuming love for God and souls. He should know these things, seeing that they must constitute the chief theme of his preaching, and that he will have to be always talking about them. But how can he be so unless he can illustrate his teaching by what has transpired in his own experience?

It follows also that officers should have in their own hearts, at the moment they are talking, the realization of the blesssings they are pushing home upon others, and it also follows that officers should mix up their own testimony with their explanations and exhortations. Paul, as a preacher, was a remarkable example in this respect. He was always giving his own experience to illustrate and enforce his doctrine. I recommend you to imitate him. I feel often when I have had to face the crowd if the people were wondering whether the things we talk about are realities with us, or whether it is all a performance or little more, and nothing is calculated to so effectually meet this difficulty as for the speaker to tell, not only what he has realized in his own heart and life of the things he is telling them about, but occasionally to describe how they came about.

Of course this method may be overdone, and an officer may describe his conversion, as any other part of his past experience, so often that the people will be nauseated. He must not do this. A word or two will usually be enough—spreading his testimony over various phases of his past life, as applied to what he is saying. For example, if you are speaking of repentance you can say how bitterly you mourned over your own sins against God and man. If you are speaking of pardon, you can tell how you found it, and of the joy that followed. If you are dwelling on a clean heart, you can tell how you entered into the land of Canaan. If you are talking about deliverance from temptation, you can tell how God has helped you to overcome, and so on. But how can you effectively describe these things to your hearers without having experienced them in your own heart and life, and how otherwise can you compel their belief than by saying, "What I publish to you I have seen and felt and enjoy myself."

> "What we have felt and seen
>   With confidence we tell
> And publish to the sons of men
>   The signs infallible"

Motivation—Speak with Conviction to Glorify God

For an officer to speak effectively, his *aim* must be right; that is to say, he must be seeking to bring men and women to God, and to make them act in harmony with their own welfare and the Divine will. That must be the purpose which influences all his preparations and performances from beginning to end. This determines his choice of a subject and songs, his choice of other speakers, the way he delivers himself, and the whole conduct of the service. His purpose all the way through is to make those present think, feel, and act according to what he feels to be their present duty to God, themselves, and those around them.

You will all know that the aim of a man in any department of life determines the character of his performance. If an officer is trying to make people admire his ability, or language, or earnestness, or anything else there is about him, that which he says and does will be with a view to the gratification of his selfish aim; whereas if he wants God to be glorified in the salvation and sanctification and inspiration of those before him, all his doing and talking will be shaped to the accomplishment of that purpose. This, too, will also govern the character of his preparation. If he does not care about saving souls, he probably will not care to prepare at all. He will waste his time in some child's play or other, or dream it away in idleness, or go to the platform and offer some meaningless talk to the people—a mere clatter of words—or hash up some stale stuff, or some old anecdotes or ideas that he has given again and again previously; or, if he is seeking to make them think he is some clever person, he will show off accordingly, and the result will answer to his aim.

The aim of an officer also determines whether the Holy Spirit shall cooperate with him. If his aim is one thing, and that of the Holy Spirit is another, there cannot be any partnership, seeing that "two cannot walk together except they be agreed" (Amos 3:3); consequently the Holy Spirit will depart or never appear. There can be no question that the reason why many officers are left without feeling or power on the platform, and often without congregations in the seats, and consequently without money and without souls, is just because the main purpose of their lives and their talking is contrary to, or, anyway, is not in unison with, that of the Divine Spirit. We know that He is seeking to glorify Jesus Christ—to exalt Him, to make Him know, to make men come to His feet and receive the blessing purchased by His blood and devote their whole beings to the extension of His kingdom on the earth—and He will only cooperate with officers where their purposes are the same.

The Need for Self Examination

Officers should be continually examining themselves on this subject, and say when they are pulling themselves together in the way of preparation for the platform, or when they open their Bibles in order to address the people, "What am I aiming at? What do I want to make these people do? Am I myself going to set forth Jesus Christ in this service? What am I seeking— the salvation of these people, or something else?" They can then determine with absolute certainty how far they have a right to claim and believe for the Holy Ghost, or how far the Holy Ghost is going to cooper- ate with them. And yet I am afraid that this self- seeking largely influences a great deal of public work in the Army. How contemptible it must appear in the sight of Jesus Christ and the angels!

For example, what should we think of the conduct of the captain of a fire brigade if he acted in a similar manner? Here is a large five-storied building in flames: the fire has got firmly hold of the lower part of the building, the people are sleeping in the higher rooms, dreaming about happy days to come; and here the fire brigade comes rattling down the streets and sets to work opposite the burning mass. Now, what should we think of a captain whose main object was to show off his engine or the capacity of his men to the crowd who stand by—to obtain admiration for their uniform; their brass helmets; their agility in climbing about; their rapidity in pouring water upon the burning building; or other matters connected with their work? The whole population would execrate it and say, "We don't want you here to show off your cleverness; we care nothing for your uniform, or anything else about you, except so far as it helps to subdue these flames and get these poor wretches out of the top stories who otherwise would be burned;" and, in fact, any man who did not make it his great business to put out the fire, would not keep his situation a week.

So, my fellow officers, your work and mine is to put out the fires in the bosoms of those round about us—consuming their happiness, time, and very souls; and to stop short of this, and be content to seek the admiration of those about us instead of seeking their salvation, must mean for us the contempt of Heaven and Hell, and drive from us the compassion of Him who sought not His own but allowed Himself to be nailed as a bloody sacrifice on the Cross.

Earnestness Necessary to Effective Preaching

By earnestness I mean that the soul of the officer should be on fire, and his whole energy engrossed with the importance of his topic. It does not follow that there must necessarily be any particular manifestations of this. A man may shout and stamp and weep and rush about in a general way, and yet not be specially in earnest. These particular developments may be a matter of habit and nothing more. Alas! alas! they sometimes are; in which case they must be peculiarly disagreeable to those who know how cold and indifferent the officer is in the usual run of his life. At the same time I must not be understood to suppose that a man can have his nature powerfully stirred on any subject, especially on religion, without some manifestation of the same. If his heart is moved at all, there will be an expression of it.

Essentials in Earnest Preaching

1. *Preach with Discernment.* In his hearers the speaker will see men and women destined to live forever, who are rebels against God and despisers of His mercy—living and dancing, buying and selling, and generally amusing themselves on the brink of hell, in danger any moment of being hurried to judgment to be condemned and damned forever. He will see it all while he is talking. All this and a great deal more will be as real to him as the material things around him.

2. *Preach with Feeling.* No man can see all these things without corresponding emotion. A blind man who skirts the precipice, or whose wife and children are doing so, will have no agony; but open his eyes, let him see the fathomless abyss at his feet, or which is threatening to swallow up his dear ones, and he will possibly die with despair. So here for the preacher; to see is to feel, to have all his energy stirred, his compassion drawn out, his intensest desires awakened, to have all stirred together at the revelation.

3. *Preach for Results.* A preacher sees the peril or the possibilities of salvation and usefulness which lie before his hearers; for example, he sees the backslider away from home, dying of hunger, ready to perish. He sees the welcome and abundance of his Father's house, and as he sees he resolves to make that prodigal return, if such a thing be within the range of possibility, and to do it there and then.

I suppose that it was this pledge of earnestness that

Jesus Christ enjoined on His disciples, and through them on their successors down the ages, in that wonderful parable in which He makes the rich man give orders to his servants *to compel* the occupants of the highways and hedges to come into his house and partake of his feast.

Without earnestness preaching cannot be said to be worthy of the name, and must inevitably fail in gaining its end. That end is the conquest of the heart, and as only the heart can speak with authority to the heart, it follows that unless the heart is in the talk it would be better not to talk at all.

Earnestness Ensures a Hearing

People will listen to a man with interest, if he is in dead earnest—if his soul is on fire with his theme— even when they totally disagree with the subject on which he speaks. How much more then, are they likely to give him careful attention when they accept the truth of what he is saying! Officers, I tell you, and I know something of this matter, that if you feel keenly the weight and burden of your speech, if lips and eyes and countenance alike testify that your soul is in what you are saying, people will listen to you out-of-doors and indoors. You will have no occasion to complain that the people will not stay to hear you in the open-air or remain until you have finished speaking in your Corps. Your knowledge and education may be very imperfect—your voice and manner may be all unattractive, but a soul on fire will make the people listen wherever you may be or whatever you may have to say.

Earnestness Will Produce Conviction.

True earnestness, comes from the heart. It appeals to the heart, and true earnestness alone can reach the heart. Skeptics and indifferentists and all sorts of doubters will believe what you say if you produce the impression that you believe it yourself. And they won't be persuaded that you believe what you are saying yourself, unless you are in earnest. But if they see your soul is in your talk, they will listen, and think, and feel, and pray, and believe, and be saved, just because they see you are a reality. But if you seem to them to be a mere parrot, or going through a performance because you think it is your duty, or that you are doing it for a living; no matter what you say, or what you do, they will regard you as a sham, and turn from you in disgust.

Earnestness Will Correct Deficiencies

It will render perfectly unnecessary much that I am writing here. An officer who is in real earnest to glorify God and save souls will, of his own instincts, do almost anything I or anyone else can suggest which has to do with efficiency as a speaker, both as to manner and matter. He will study his Bible and his own heart, and range through all heaven and earth and hell to find arguments and reasons calculated to induce men and women to forsake sin and the devil, to accept mercy and enter the Kingdom of Heaven, and when he has found arguments he will deliver them with the most tremendous effect right into the very souls of those who hear him.

Oh, this earnestness is a great gift, and a mighty force in the Salvation war, I assure you. Alas, alas, it is none too plentiful; but where possessed, it should be nursed, and fed, and cared for as a great treasure; and where not possessed, it should be sought with tears, and prayers, and every other means that are calculated to obtain it. I would sooner have one simple minded man or woman to help me in this struggle with evil and the powers of darkness whose soul is *red hot with burning zeal* even if he does not know a letter in a book, and therefore has never read a passage in the Bible, than fifty people full of book lore and the learning of the schools without it. My poor unlettered man would soon learn all he needs for the gathering of thousands to Christ; whereas the fifty whose heads are full of knowledge and "great thoughts" (as they call them) and of conceit as to their ability, while their hearts are empty of this holy flame, would go from town to town leaving the track of darkness and desolation and backsliding and failure behind them.

Earnestness Will Bring Inspiration

The larger proportion of the few soldiers who have cast in their lot with Jesus Christ are a nervous and timid set with respect to daring and desperate action. They are frightened at their own shadow and everlastingly suffering from a miserable fear either of displeasing God, or their own selves, or someone else.

The value and importance of men whose inward sense of the reality and importance of Divine things over-powers the fear of man and consequences, and who can rush forward to the discharge of duty at all risks, cannot be measured. They not only convince the nervous, frightened soldiers of the Cross, but carry them with them, lead them in the fight, compel their admiration and imitation, and so transform them into warriors as brave and as daring as themselves. Earnest men lead the race and rule the world. As we want the race to be led to Christ, and the world to be saved and purified by His blood, we want earnest officers.

Faith in God means faith in the word He has spoken, but it means more than that; it means confidence in God Himself. So that when things are happening around you that appear to be opposed to the notion that God is kindly disposed toward you, you must believe that He is loving you all the time, and that He is really making all things work together for your good.

. . . William Booth

CHAPTER II

The Preparation of Sermons

SHOULD I prepare for the platform beforehand? is a question, I fancy many officers have frequently asked themselves, and to which question some at least have never received a satisfactory answer. I confess to having in early life frequently been troubled with the same inquiry, and for a long time was not a little perplexed. I have long since, however, decided upon what is the Lord's will with respect to my own practice, and although I cannot say that I am able to speak as to what should absolutely be the practice of others, I can give my judgment, and officers must decide for themselves.

The most powerful preachers I have known personally, or by reputation, with only one or two exceptions, have been in the habit of making some preparation beforehand. The most effective preacher by far that I came across in my youth, the great revivalist the Rev. James Caughey, prepared most carefully, although in no way allowing himself to be in bondage to what he had gathered beforehand.

Of course you will know that I should condemn at the outset, and that most strongly, any preparation prompted by any other purpose than that already described. The same single aim, *God and Souls,* which regulates a man's work on the platform, must guide and govern him in the preparation he makes for it, and I cannot see why a man may not walk about his room, or sit down to his table and say,

"Oh, God, I am going to that meeting tonight to talk about the duty those deathless souls owe to Thee, to each other, and to mankind. Some of them are traveling to hell, nay, may be at this hour on its very brink. I want to persuade them to flee from the wrath to come by submitting to Thy authority and plunging into the fountain of Jesus' blood. Oh, help me, Thou blessed Spirit, by giving me thoughts and words that will awaken these sleepers, carry conviction to their hearts, and bring them to salvation."

I say, I cannot see any reason why God should not answer that prayer as to what I should say to them, by giving light and leading before the time, as truly as at the hour that I rise to speak.

In addition, it does not seem to be unreasonable that I should make calls upon the truths stored up in my memory, look into my Bible, and even seek for explanations on topics which at the first blush appear dark and difficult from the inspired teaching of other men of God.

Preparation is in harmony with human reason and human action. Men prepare carefully when they want to secure any earthly results. To produce a crop, the farmer prepares the ground for the seed, and prepares the seed before he casts it into the earth.

To effect a cure, the doctor studies the special characteristics of disease, the condition and circumstances of his patients, and refers to the action of other physicians in similar cases.

To obtain a satisfactory verdict, the lawyer studies his case, examines his witnesses, hunts up his arguments, and considers how he is going to order all before the court.

I want to secure a harvest of souls for my Master. I want to effect the care of the diseased-stricken people who sit before me, and to obtain a verdict from my audience in favor of truth and the claims of Jesus Christ, and it seems only reasonable that I should make such preparation beforehand as will enable me to gain my end and bring conviction to the hearts and consciences of those with whom I have to do.

But it may be said, did not Christ make an express promise bearing upon this question? Did He not say, *"But when they shall lead you, and deliver you up, take no thought beforehand what ye shall speak, neither do ye premeditate; but whatsoever shall be given you in that hour, that speak ye, for it is not ye that speak, but the Holy Ghost"* (Mark 13:11).

What does this mean that is promised here? I may say at once, that there is room to question whether this passage refers to preaching in the ordinary sense at all. It simply signifies that when ignorant people are brought before rulers for professing the faith of

Jesus Christ, that the Holy Spirit in their hearts will teach them what to say.

For instance, here is a poor woman, or young girl, seized and dragged to prison, and charged with the offence of praying to Jesus Christ. Anxious not only to defend herself, but to speak for her Master and for the benefit of His enemies, how could she tell what to say on such an occasion? The circumstances would be altogether new to her. Probably she has never been in a Court of Justice before, knowing nothing of its forms or usages; therefore, no amount of labor or thought on her account would be of any avail. She could make no preparation if she would. Consequently Jesus Christ relieved her from all responsibility on the subject by saying, *"And when they bring you unto the synagogues, and unto magistrates, and powers, take ye no thought how or what thing ye shall answer, or what ye shall say: For the Holy Ghost shall teach you in the same hour what ye ought to say"* (Luke 12:11, 12).

Now I am not going to say that the blessed Spirit does not help Salvation Army officers at the very hour when they are talking, and give them words to say to the people direct from the Throne. I believe He does. I believe, as I have said elsewhere, that as holy men of old spake as the Spirit gave them utterance, so He still inspires holy men of modern times with suitable words and arguments.

I believe He frequently pours through me words of burning truth into the ears and hearts of those who hear me—words that I have not the remotest idea beforehand that I am going to use, and words which, if I would, I could never call up to memory to use again. I believe that He has been dealing with me after this fashion during these last few months perhaps as never before, and yet I feel constrained, so far as my own practice is concerned, to ask Him beforehand to give me some idea of what He would have me say to the people; nay, I feel constrained to use such powers as He has given me, and to call to my aid such knowledge as I possess beforehand, in order to shape thoughts and illustrations and scriptures in such form as shall seem most likely to glorify His dear name and bring lost sinners to His feet.

If He sent me to seek a lost sheep in the wilderness, or to pull an ox out of some pit into which he had stumbled in the night, I should endeavor to gain any information not already in my possession which my employer might possess concerning the duty which he commissioned me to discharge, and I should equally endeavor to use such measures as I was already familiar with and which seemed appropriate to the occasion. He has sent me to seek lost men and women and children wandering in the wilderness of sin and misery, and to pull the wretched backsliders and drunkards and harlots out of the horrible pit into which they have fallen, and to stimulate all true blood-and-fire soldiers to take part in the same blessed task; and while relying on Him for the supply of that wisdom and strength which I possess not, I still feel that it is only reasonable that I should use such knowledge, such arguments, such words, such songs, and such other measures as I already have knowledge of, or which I can by thought and inquiry obtain, and which appear likely to secure the accomplishment of my end.

The Sermon Itself

1. *Don't Make Sermonettes Which Conclude with a Weak Application.* By a sermonette I mean a speech about some passage of Scripture, or some occurrence in New or Old Testament history, with an application to your audience made at the close, or in the middle, or not at all, the whole of which has no direct or immediate application to the present salvation and sanctification, and inspiration with a red-hot religion, of the people who are before you.

2. *Don't Get up Anything Like a Speech,* such as a lot of sentences strung together to be memorized, and said to a congregation like a schoolboy says his piece. I call that spouting; and anything like spouting is objectionable. Words, whether many or few, committed to memory and repeated over and over again are, as a rule, hateful—especially on a Salvation Army platform, or, as far as that goes, anywhere else. All preachments lose their power over their hearers by repetition, and that simply because they lose their hold upon the mind of the speaker. The life goes out of them that they had at birth, and they become dead things; and nobody likes to have death hawked about before them, whether in the name of religion or anything else.

A few memorized opening sentences may be excusable sometimes with beginners, especially if they are very nervous and timid. It may help to create confidence; but even this is sometimes objectionable. Better by far to get your own ideas well into your head, and trust in God for language.

Therefore, beware of making addresses of the "patchwork" school, composed of alternate texts, books, and other people's thoughts, and anecdotes in general.

3. *Beware of Simply Preparing with a View to Show Off Your Ability in Any Respect Whatever.*

4. *Beware of Going to the Platform with Anything That Will Interfere with Your Perfect Freedom of Spirit,* or bar the way to the fullest communication by the Holy Ghost of ideas to your heart at the moment, or to any leading or teaching you may get from the people before you, during the progress of the meeting, or from the circumstances of the hour.

The Preacher Himself

There is a preparation beyond any mere gathering together of ideas, which appears to me to be of even greater importance than that to which I have already referred. In order to speak effectively of the things of the Kingdom, the soul of the speaker must be wide awake to their importance, and to the responsibility of the opportunity presented at the moment when he endeavors to speak on them. Men's minds and hearts go to sleep as truly as their bodies. Officers may be moving about and talking and acting outwardly, while the inner man is at least three parts asleep. The duty of dealing with men about their souls and the great realities of the eternal world are so immensely important, that every officer ought to come up to it with every faculty sensitive and active to the fullest extent.

Many officers who read this will doubtless remember wonderful times of liberty and power enjoyed on certain occasions in the past when great troubles had befallen them. They have gone to the platform feeling totally unequal to the task, crushed down and broken-hearted, feeling that they ought not to be called upon to the sacred business of comforting or saving or improving others while in such a condition of mind and heart. To their surprise, however, and the surprise of everyone around them, they have been lifted up above their own mournful experience and talked like angels from heaven. The reason has simply been that their souls have been properly awakened and they have talked more effectively in consequence. Just as they would have done better in a business transaction when properly alive to the chance of making a good bargain, than they would when tired out and half asleep.

1. *The Importance of Prayer.* Here is an indirect benefit of incalculable worth. The soul that rises up to wrestle with God for His blessing on a forthcoming effort, not only secures an answer in the direct pouring out of the Holy Ghost on his own soul, and the co-operating influences on the hearts of his hearers, but

has all the latent energies of his own spirit roused up thereby. The inward perception he attains of Divine things, the sight of Calvary and the Judgment Day, and of heaven and hell, the blessedness of salvation, and the terribleness of damnation, all tend together to stir his whole being, and send him to the platform or the streets with every spiritual instinct all alive, and his whole nature full of nervous energy equal to every emergency.

2. *Lessons from Open-Air Ministry.* Nothing is much better calculated to wake up the officer for his work on the platform than a good open-air fight. Direct communion with the outer world in the streets and drinking saloons will move the soul to its very depths. Hearing the crowd blaspheme his Master and curse his religion, and seeing the multitudes rushing down to hell, will bring him to the front ready to do the very best that lies in his power.

Some years back a Roman Catholic priest was moving all Paris by his powerful, pathetic preaching in the great cathedral of Notre Dame. The people came in thousands, waited for hours, and groaned and sobbed aloud while he talked about the sufferings of Jesus Christ, the terribleness of sin, and judgment and hell. This priest, prior to entering the pulpit, was accustomed to descend into the vaults under the cathedral, and was there, by his own choice and in-structions, suspended by some of his colleagues to a real cross and beaten with rods for the space of half an hour in order that he might be the better prepared to speak to the people by some actual realization of what his Master had suffered on their behalf.

Now I don't recommend any officer follow this example with his body, but I do say that it would be good and profitable to him and his people if he should in spirit commune and sympathize and suffer with his Lord, and that he should go out and look at the multitudes who are perishing around him after the same fashion that his Master did, and by every possible method arouse his soul to the realization of the solemn responsibilities devolving upon him in standing up between the living and the dead and delivering His message to dying men.

But let me come now to the officer on the platform, whether the platform be in the Corps or out of it. For all I have said or have to say has, and will have, I hope, an equal application to the work of talking to the people whether it be done indoors or out of doors. God forbid that I should leave the open-airs out of my calculations; for, so far as I can see, the great battles of the future will be fought in the open-air. Every day shows a greater indisposition on the part of the masses to cross the threshold of any building, whatever name it may bear, if they have any apprehension that the plain, burning truths which lead to the salvation of the soul are going to be spoken there. Therefore it follows, that if the people will not come to us, the greater is the necessity and urgency that will be laid upon us to go to them. And to them we Salvationists must and will go.

The
Topic

BY a topic I mean some particular subject to which you shall specially address yourself; and the sort of subject you want is one that has to do with the present duty of those who will hear you; only that kind of subject is worthy of a Salvation Army officer or suited to a Salvation Army platform. We have no time for theorizing, or speculation, or general talk. Beware of the habit of saying that which means nothing in particular, and which, although delivered with plenty of energy and sound and outward earnestness, has no meaning of any special importance. Now, what ought your topic to be?

Contains Important Truth

It should contain some truth which will cling to the memories of your hearers if everything you say about it is forgotten. I have often observed, in my own experience, that a much greater effect has been produced by some definite heavy truth, even when I have been greatly restricted in talking about it, than has seemed to be the case when I have had great liberty of speech and much acceptance with the people on some topic that has not of itself been so important. For instance, no officer can talk about such subjects as "The Evil of Sin Here and Hereafter;" "Salvation to the Uttermost;" "Purity of Heart;" "The Universal Obligation of Every Soldier to Live and Fight and Die for Christ;" "The Hour of Death;" "The Judgment Day;" "The Sorrows of Lost Souls" or any other kindred themes, without producing a great impression, if the Holy Spirit is with him, however imperfectly he may discharge his task.

Avoid the Familiar

Don't talk any more than is necessary about such truths as all are familiar with, and which all profess to believe. That truth which is most uncommon will be most useful. For instance, the immense bulk of the people who attend our meetings readily admit the willingness of God to save them, and are perfectly aware of the freeness, fulness, and sufficiency of Salvation. In fact, the willingness of God to save is, with the multitudes, the reason why they go on sinning, hence time is all but thrown away in pressing these subjects upon them. The sin of the regular salvation hearer and of multitudes outside our ranks is that of presumption. They think that God is so anxious to save them, that they do not need to have the slightest fear of being damned. They consider that they will only have to kneel down and offer a short prayer, or sit down and believe some passage of Scripture, in order to be made perfectly secure for both time and eternity.

There is, therefore, not so much need for any officer to spend his time and strength in setting forth the willingness and ability of God to save. On the contrary, let him show the danger there is of these people being forsaken by the Spirit—sinning away the day of grace —having the things which belong to their peace forever hidden from their eyes, as was the case with the Jews, being suddenly taken away to death; or let him picture them crying for mercy when Christ won't hear them.

Apply to Your People

You want a subject—a subject that has to do with the present salvation of those very people who will hear you. You want to help them to get saved, to overcome their evil habits, to master the devils with whom they have to fight, and to set them on to fight for God themselves if they have not yet begun to do so.

Attract the Outsiders

The announcement of it will serve as an advertisement. Then let me caution you to beware of what is merely sensational. I don't care how strongly or strangely it may strike the people beforehand if you can only turn it to good account. Many years ago, when stationed as a minister in the north of England, and casting about for some subject that would draw a crowd, I announced from the pulpit that on the following Sabbath I would preach the "Funeral Sermon of All the Saints that Had Gone from Gateshead to

Heaven During the Last Thirty years." The subject came on and brought the people in all directions, and we had a good time and a number of penitents. I then announced that on the following Sunday I would preach "A Funeral Service for All the Sinners who Had Gone from Gateshead to Hell during the last Thirty Years." We had on this occasion another packed house and more penitents. Now here are sensational subjects, but they are such as were easily made to tell in favor of salvation there and then.

Immediate Action the Goal

You must always keep this in view. This purpose alone will determine the difference between you and ordinary sermonizers. They are content with a discourse that explains some doctrine, or sets forth some duty, or illustrates some piece of biblical history, or something else of the same kind. Not so you; your aim is to bring the very rebels against God who sit before you to His feet there and then; to make those who have already submitted themselves to His control better and happier and holier and more useful—and you want them to decide in favor of these things during that service. Your topic must therefore be such as will lead up to this.

Finding the Topic

How am I to discover such a subject? I reply, hunt about for it. Pearls are not always found lying about your feet; they are only found after a search, they will pay for it when found. Just so with useful topics.

1. *Ask God.* Begin always, whether at home or abroad or on the platform, at the right place; and the right place for information as well as for help is the mercy-seat. Ask the Holy Spirit to guide you.

2. *Anticipate the Character of Your Audience.* If you are a stranger, inquire. With respect to an audience I invariably ask those who are familiar with the people to tell me its character. It would be ridiculous for me to go off speaking to people as to their duty without knowing their condition. We should think a doctor mad who went into a hospital and began to give orders right away for the distribution of medicine, bandages and the like among the patients without first inquiring carefully into the condition of each. While we cannot always know or learn the exact spiritual state of every hearer, we can readily ascertain something as to their general condition, and fix our topic and our treatment of it accordingly.

Supposing that the bulk or any considerable proportion of your audience is composed of unconverted people, your subject must be adapted to them. Nay, if any considerable number consists of the unsaved, you will give them the preference. I always feel constrained to do so; they are most needy, and I must go, not only to those who need me, but to those who need me most.

If they are soldiers, then you want a topic suited to them. That settles the general character of your theme, but you should be more particular still.

You must consider the present time condition of

your hearers. It is not enough to find out the general divisions of character. As, for instance, whether saints or sinners. If unconverted, are they instructed in religion? Are they Gospel hardened? Are there many backsliders among them? or are they utter neglecters of salvation? or, if saved, what is their particular state. Discover and fix your subject accordingly.

3. *Seize upon Remarkable Events.* Such events may be occupying the public mind; such as a great fire, a mine accident, a notorious crime, a shipwreck or any other similar occurrence. Such events will attract the multitude, command the attention of an audience from the onset, and from them any number of telling illustrations can be drawn. Officers should keep their eyes open, seize upon these passing occurrences, and use them to drive the truth home to the hearts of the people.

Developing the Topic

When a subject is first suggested to my own mind it will often be all confusion. I am probably able to see something in it that is likely to be effective, but the difficulty is, how to get it into such a shape that my audience will understand its meaning, feel its importance, see its application to them, and be induced by it to act as I wish. Here is a difficulty, as I have already remarked, when this topic walks into my mind and takes hold of my imagination I cannot always at first sight see how it is going to be dealt with.

Very often after turning it over once or twice I am

hopeless. The subject loses rather than gains upon me. The charm it had for me at the onset fades away and I dismiss it. But then it will come back again, bringing some new light with it as to its management, and seeming to say "You must use me."

I then grapple with it, turning it over and over, thinking about it when I go to sleep, and when I wake, in the night, as I dress, in the train, and as I walk about. Gradually it begins to assume a possible shape; I get out my notebook and write about it. Illustrations rise up to clothe it, and finally I am able to pour it out upon the people, and have the joy of seeing crowds of saints and sinners drawn to seek God by it.

I don't say that I always have this difficulty; sometimes, nay very often, a subject rises up all unsought, and unfolds itself without the asking. This will frequently be the case when I am otherwise engaged, and should always be secured at the moment by being written down in some sort of a notebook for further service.

But the question which I am now supposing to be asked by an officer is, How am I to deal with a topic when I have got one? In other words, How can I present a given subject to an audience so as to produce the result I want? In trying to answer this question I don't forget that I am writing to cadets and young officers, and thus those of my readers who are old hands must not overlook the necessity I am under of giving counsels that may seem very elementary in their character.

In dealing with a topic, I think you will very often be much helped by proposing some simple questions to it such as the following:

1. What does the subject mean?

2. Why ought we to do it? What arguments are there in the Bible, in experience, in this world or the next, why this duty should be attended to?

3. How is this duty to be discharged? or, How is this experience to be gained? or, How is this blessing to be enjoyed? or, What are the conditions which have to be performed before this blessing can be obtained?

4. When ought this work to be done?

Now these and similar questions, which will readily occur to you upon a little thought will help you to see into a subject. They will also help to make it plain to your own mind and to the minds of your hearers.

Let me see if I can illustrate. Take any ordinary topic, such as Holiness, the Forgiveness of Sins, the Uncertainty of Life, Repentance, Faith, Judgment, Heaven, Hell, or any other, and apply this plan.

We will take Repentance for instance. How will you deal with it? You will begin by asking the question, What is it? What does repenting of your sins mean? The answer will come back to any cadet that repentance must mean, among other things:

a. Feeling yourself a sinner.

b. Hating your sins and giving them up: that is, promising never to commit them any more.

c. It must mean asking God for forgiveness and aid.

d. It must mean believing that God means what He says when He offers to forgive you, and it must mean that such forgiveness is accepted with all the heart.

Why ought we to repent? And such reasons will come back as:

a. Because it is so wicked to sin against a God who is so good, so loving, and so compassionate.

b. Because salvation is impossible without forgiveness. A father cannot forgive his boy who has been disobedient, however anxious he may be to do so, until the boy sees his wrong-doing, and is sorry for it, and promises to do so no more. And just so it must be with your Heavenly Father.

c. If sinners do not repent here, where forgiveness may be obtained, they will repent in eternity, where there will be no salvation.

How must this duty be discharged? That is, how must he repent? And the answer will come back:

a. That he must look at his sins until he feels how hateful they are.

b. He must go down before God, there and then, at the penitent-form or somewhere else, and confess them, and tell God he will give them up and accept salvation on the spot.

Supposing an officer wants to refer to some event, such as the loss of the "Victoria" of which the people's minds are so full at the present moment. I think it will help him if he asks some such questions as the following:

a. What remarkable features does this calamity present?
b. What lesson does it teach? What is there to learn from it that has to do with the present and everlasting salvation of the people?
c. How can I by it illustrate and bring home to my hearers their present duty in relation to God, themselves, or their fellow men?

Now, I don't think any officer would find any difficulty in working out this plan, and the more practice he has the more readily will he be able to do so. Let him do everything in the spirit of prayer and dependence upon the Holy Ghost, and God will help him.

Summary

The speaker should always keep three things in view in all his preparation for the platform:

1. He, himself, should be careful to understand what he is going to say to other people. If he doesn't how can he expect other people to understand him? He should think, and pray and read his Bible, until all is plain to his own mind, and then he will be likely to make it plain to others.

2. He should illustrate plentifully. That is, he should compare the subject which he is endeavoring to make his hearers understand with some simple things of everyday occurrence with which they are familiar.

3. He should apply everything as he goes along to the heart and conscience of his hearers. He must drive home the truth or it will be useless. He must be continually saying, *"You are the people whom this concerns"* or they will put it from them and not feel that it means them. He should do this all the way through. He cannot afford, like the ordinary sermoniser, to make a long exposition and then have a little application at the close. He must go for the heart at every turn.

*And now, Hallelujah! the rest
of my days
Shall gladly be spent in
promoting His praise
Who opened His bosom to pour
out this sea
Of boundless salvation for
you and for me.*

. . . William Booth

CHAPTER IV

Delivering the Message

I WANT to give some suggestions that shall be more strictly suitable and more immediately useful to officers in speaking to the people. We will suppose he has got his message, at least some part of it. *How Shall He Deliver That Message?*

Be Natural

Be natural in the way you talk. Be yourself, struggle to forget even yourself; that is, to lose yourself in the discharge of your duty. While you are thinking about yourself, or rather of what the people may think about you, or of what you are going to say next, or about anything but the salvation of the people before you, you will be hindered, if not actually disqualified, for your duty. Throw yourself into the fight regardless of anything and everything. Never mind what sort of a spectacle you make. Give yourself up to the task of securing victory, and you will be very likely to gain it.

Be natural with regard to what you say as well as to the way you say it. Don't spout other people's compositions. Use their ideas and illustrations to any extent you think will be likely to be useful, but put them through your own mill first. Eat them and digest them with your brains. Take them in and deal with them much as you do your food, and then they will come from you as much alive as your own original thoughts and feelings.

Don't Imitate

Don't imitate others, however much you may admire them, or however useful they may be. Even if you could acquire what is best in their manner of saying and doing things, it is very improbable whether you would be likely to be more useful than you will be in acting out your own original self. But imitators of other speakers in manner or voice are usually worse rather than better for it, seeing that they ordinarily acquire the most objectionable features of the person they copy.

In my native town at one time there was a certain minister who was very useful, and consequently very popular. Crowds flocked to hear him, and many souls were saved. There was also a certain local preacher there who also wanted to be useful, and who thought the best thing he could do to accomplish this was to copy this minister. Consequently he adopted his voice and manners as nearly as he could, and sallied forth to a neighboring village, dressed in his borrowed clothes. But the simple villagers were not captivated, and sent him a kind message at the close of the day to the effect that they did not like him nearly as well with John Smith's coat on as his own.

Talk Colloquially

By this I mean, talk naturally, just as you talk at the table or in conversation. Don't imagine that you have to shout or to use some sort of platform twang. It is astonishing how interesting some people are in private conversation, and how utterly uninteresting they become directly they mount the platform. This is largely because they go off into some unnatural way of speaking.

Talk With Your Tongue

Don't scrape your throat, or drag your words up from your chest. It is quite painful to hear some people rasp their poor throats, and pump their words up out of their stomachs until you expect they are going to roll over or go off into a fit. This makes killing work of talking, and no wonder that officers who have fallen into this habit are so soon exhausted. If you have contracted this method of speaking, and don't feel free with any other, of course you must go on with it I suppose, for nothing must be allowed to destroy your freedom when engaged in your duty.

Talking in a natural manner is ordinarily a healthy exercise, and a man ought to be able, so far as the mere physical exertion of speaking is concerned, to be able to use his tongue without injury to himself so long as he can use his arms and legs. We see this to be so in the case of street peddlers and others who sell their goods in the open air. They go on day by day, and usually thrive with the practice . . . .

Talk to Your Audience

Talk to the people who are before you. Take in their characters as you mount the platform and your eye first looks over them. If you don't know them, inquire from those who do, and then go for them. Never mind what preparation you may have made, or what preconceived form of speech or service you may have thought about; *there* is your work. You have to influence, and move, and instruct those very people who are standing in that crowd and sitting on those seats looking up into your face. You have to make them think, and feel, and act in that manner which will please God and secure their salvation, and if possible you have to do it there and then.

Now look at them. It is not whether you can please them, send them away satisfied, get a good collection, induce them to come again; the first and foremost thing with you is to save and sanctify and inspire them with the burning love of Jesus Christ.

This is your time, my comrades. Cry to God to help you, and look these people in the eyes, and make them feel that you are speaking to them, and that you understand how they are fixed, what they are thinking about, the sins they are guilty of, the habits that bind them, the difficulties that lie in the way of their salvation, and the working of the great remedy that you set before them.

Talk to them in as straight a manner as you would if you had them one by one in your own quarters, and were reasoning with them personally. To be able to do that is almost the perfection of preaching. No higher compliment than the following was ever paid to preachers than that to which, thank God, we Salvationists are not strangers. "I went into the Corps a stranger to the officer on the platform and the people around me, but he seemed to set his eyes on me and to talk to me all the time, and in such a way that I felt sure someone must have been telling him all about my past life." Oh, that is the talking of the heart to the heart!

Be in Good Physical Condition

Go to the platform in as good a physical condition as you can. The close connection existing between the state of the body and the mind is well known. Good spirits are a wonderful qualification for freedom and effectiveness in speaking, while a languid condition of body, or a stomach out of order, are uncompromising enemies of good spirits as they are indeed of almost every other grace.

Now, while health and physical vigor are not at our command, I know that it is possible to do much in that direction. See how the athletes train themselves. How careful they are in what they eat and drink; in exercising themselves, and in the amount of sleep they take, striving by all means within their power to come up to their work in what they call "good condition."

I will illustrate here with my own experience. I have to take all manner of care to keep myself equal to my work. I have to guard my appetites and rigidly refuse even the slightest indulgences that would be likely to disorder my stomach or depress my nervous powers. Nay, as a rule, I find that anything like a full or satisfying meal immediately before I speak, hinders my ease and comfort in speaking. My experience may be no criterion on which to guide others, but I give it for what it is worth, and I have heard other speakers of prominence say substantially the same. Every man who wants to get the greatest amount of work out of his body, brain, and heart, for the sake of the Kingdom of God and the salvation of souls, will have to study himself and act with care. I am sure you will bear with me in saying here that I fear that much time is lost on the sick list, and that many nervous prostrations and breakdowns, and, if I am not mistaken, many early graves are the result of ill-management in eating and drinking, and in the management of the body generally.

Be Conscious of Deportment

No one who knows me will suppose for a moment that I have any partiality to anything like a melancholy or sanctimonious manner in a speaker, whether on the platform, in the open-air or anywhere else. A hard, cold, funereal style, or anything approaching to it will of itself be sufficient to close the ears and hearts of the people against you, while a warm, friendly manner of address is indispensable if you are to be listened to by the crowds whom you want to interest, benefit, and save.

At the same time I want to say that I am equally

opposed to anything after the fun-making style, and therefore warn every officer against being led away into the habit of joking or retailing jests, the saying of silly and ridiculous things, simply for the purpose of making people laugh or amusing them for the moment.

If you were a clown in a circus ring, put there on purpose to amuse an audience, it would be quite a different thing; your hearers would have come on purpose to be amused, and have paid for it, and you would be a buffoon paid to furnish them with the article. But your case is altogether different. The men and women before you are rebels against God, on the verge of hell. Mercy is offered them. They are indifferent to the offer. You are sent of God, or profess to be, to impress them with their danger and to persuade them to accept the offered grace and flee from the wrath to come.

On the other hand, your hearers will be the children of God, pressed down by the troubles of life, perplexed with its difficulties, endangered by its temptations, or depressed and discouraged by ten thousand things that are calculated to lessen their zeal in the great war against evil. In which case your calling from God and man, from earth and heaven, evidently is to seriously and earnestly help them as they need to the uttermost of your ability.

Now, officers should try to note the difference between what is simply natural or humorous, and what is jocose or laughable. I fancy that mistakes are frequently made because this distinction is not observed. Character may be described so exactly and so natural- ly by a speaker that it is impossible to avoid smiling on the part of the hearers; or the truth, the plainest truth, the most cutting truth, may be put before people in such a pleasant and simple manner that it amuses them while it convicts and condemns them at every turn. The pleasant manner only acts as a feather which carries the arrow more surely and deeply to the heart.

But all this is quite a different thing to officers say- ing funny or silly things just to make people laugh, or to create an agreeable sensation for the moment. That I am compelled utterly to condemn, nay, I go further, and say that no officer should be tempted to raise any merry and hilarious spirit in any audience without being able to immediately follow it up with some correspondingly weighty truth. Before the smile has died away from the countenance the Sword of the Spirit should be plunged into the heart. For, under no circumstances, can there be any reasonable excuse for the saying or doing anything while engaged in so serious a business, and speaking on so solemn and important a subject, which does not contain some useful lesson, or prepare the way for some divinely inspired truth.

I should think, if there is one sight which above another excites the deepest abhorrence of the angels, as they flit about this world on their errands of mercy, it is to see a man or woman doing the buffoon in the pulpit, or on the platform while professing to represent the suffering, agonizing Christ, whose whole life was a sorrow, and whose death filled heaven with silence and awe. When you are tempted, as tempted you will be, to jest simply to gain the smiles of your audience, remember Him and His history, and forbear!

Brother, sister, settle it forever in your soul that to be effective it is essential that those who hear you should feel that you are in dead earnest, that you are sent of God and talking for eternity; and never forget that jesting or silly talking will utterly prevent the formation of such a conviction, or effectually destory it if it is already there.

Be Heard

Speak up! Make everybody hear you, and that if you can without any effort to themselves. When you stand up to speak, always remember that your business is to convey some particular ideas to the minds and hearts of the people before you, with a view to their being influenced thereby. But what you say will be of no service unless it can be heard, and that readily. Many who will be at the trouble to come to your Corps will not be at much trouble either to hear or under-stand what you have to say when they are there unless they can do it with ease. To this end stand with your head well up, and pitch your voice so that you feel yourself that those in the further seats can hear you.

Don't speak louder than is necessary for this. To do so will neither make it pleasanter for them to listen, nor easier for you to speak. Any amount of voice more than is necessary to be heard means, on your part, just that much strength thrown away. Moreover, if you shout all the way through your address, you cannot raise your voice without some unpleasant shriek or scream when you come to the more important parts of it which you will want to emphasize.

Some speakers fall into an objectionable habit of commencing their addresses in a low, muttering key, and rise as they warm to their subject, as they call it. This may be a necessity for them, and very agreeable to those on the front seats who can hear what you say; but it appears to me to be very unfair to those further down the building who cannot hear, and who have consequently to wait for the "warming-up process" before they know what is really going on. Avoid this custom, which is a horrid one in my estimation. Stand up at the onset and make yourself heard by everyone in the building.

Be Understood

Make yourself understood when you are heard. As you cannot benefit your hearers by anything you say unless they hear your words, even so your words will be of no service unless your hearers know their meaning, or grasp the ideas that you intend to convey to them.

This applies to your *language*. Avoid the use of hard words even if they are natural to you, much more don't try to find them. In the first place, the people who do understand your fine language won't think you any the cleverer for it, but just the contrary; and those who don't understand it will be effectually hindered from gaining any benefit by what you say. Hard words and ponderous high-flown sentences are directly opposed to effective speaking. The most powerful orators the world has ever known have used the simplest language. In modern times I may instance John Bright in the political, and Charles Spurgeon in the religious world. Both these men, each standing at the head of his order, so far as Great Britain is concerned, seldom used words that were above the comprehension of the most ordinary individual in their meetings.

For myself, I purposely select the simplest language that I can possibly command, never knowingly using a word that appears above the apprehension of the youngest and most unlearned of my audience, and when by any means such a word does slip from my tongue I invariably follow it in explanation with one that can be readily understood.

Many people don't understand hard words because they have never had the privilege of education; and many who have spent years in the ordinary public schools, are perfectly ignorant of the meaning of many of the words that are in use around them everyday. Then many of your hearers have never been to school at all, and you are bound by the mere feeling of benevolence to use such language as they can readily apprehend. What possible profit can there be to these poor creatures if you don't?

A story comes to my memory in illustration of this that I remember hearing when a boy. A certain clergyman had been preaching an occasional sermon at the church of a friend where the audience was largely made up of working people. When the company sat down after the service to dinner at the parsonage, something was said about the sermon, and the vicar suggested to his visitor that he was afraid that it was very much over the heads of the congregation. The strange clergyman was very much surprised, and said he thought he had been very simple, and asked if any words could be named that he had employed which could not be readily understood. "Well," said the vicar, "you talked about 'drawing an inference' and I fancy there were a good many in the church this morning who would not know what that meant." The stranger, surprised, said he could not believe it. To test the matter it was agreed that the vicar should call in his driver and ascertain whether he understood the meaning of the phrase.

Accordingly the driver came in, and the vicar said, "Well, John, I want to ask you a question" "Right,'sir!" "Do you think, John," the vicar went on, "that you could draw and inference?" Whereupon John scratch his head, thought for a time and then replied, "Well, sir, I guess that our grey mare could draw anything that the harness would hold." The company smiled, John retired, and the strange parson was convinced that he had been using language which his audience could not comprehend. Mind you don't go over the heads of the poor people whose salvation or damnation depends on your making matters plain to them, by using words they cannot understand.

Don't labor to say things upon your subject that have never been said before, or to say them in some unusual manner. Your business is not to make an exhibition of fireworks by using such curious language, or sounding sentences that have never been listened to by your hearers, thereby exciting their wonder and admiration of your ability, but to distribute the bread of life, and to persuade the perishing people to eat of it. Or, varying the figure, you are not sent by God to gain the admiration of the people who are dying all around of the hell-plague of sin, but to persuade them to gaze upon the Crucified and be healed.

Be simple and understandable in your ideas. The Way of Salvation, and everything that has to do with walking in it, and with all the deep and experimental blessedness to which it leads, both in this life and in the next, is so simple that a fool, though a wayfaring man, can understand it if placed before him in a simple, straightforward and understandable manner.

Now, I don't know how to be sufficiently emphatic here. In talking about preparation I have to some extent gone over this ground, but I must refer to it again. To be successful you must be understood. I am quite sure that we are always falling into the mistake of supposing that our hearers know more about the things concerning the Kingdom of God than they do. Nothing is much more puzzling to me than the ignorance of people who have been hearing salvation preaching for a lifetime, respecting the simplest questions connected with religion. They are as dark in many places as the very heathen concerning the meaning of forgiveness, and faith, and holiness, and the love of Christ, and the evils of sin, the joys of Heaven and the pains of Hell. How much more ignorant must those multitudes be who have had scarcely any teaching at all on these subjects!

Then it must be remembered that it is not merely intellectual ignorance that we have to fight; it is the natural darkness and pollution of the human heart, and the devices, excuses and misrepresentations which the devil only too often whispers into one ear while we in the name of Jesus Christ are speaking to the other; for Satan fights with us for the souls of men at every turn.

We must therefore set ourselves, when we stand up to talk to the people, to be as simple as simplicity itself. We must understand what we want to say ourselves, and then say it in the plainest possible language and make ourselves understood if necessary by going over and over again with it.

In talking to an audience you should carefully watch the countenance of your hearers. You can readily gather from their faces whether they understand you or not, and if you feel they don't you must try again, for, whatever happens, you must be understood.

Section Two

But beware, O my Soul, beware of despising the day of small and feeble things. You won't get everything on a magnificent scale. Thousands will not comprise your audiences nor hundreds flock . . . every night. But let us be thankful for the bruised reed and the smoking flax, and mind that we do not break the one nor quench the other . . . and see to it that we do the work given us to do with all our might and that we do it well. Ten thousand Hallelujahs for all the past, and Unswerving Faith for the Future!

. . . William Booth

Part I

SUMMARY

FROM the foregoing, one is quickly aware of the Founder's passion for the souls of sinful mankind. Nothing is to stand in the way of presenting the gospel message of Jesus Christ in a manner to be understood by everyone in the audience.

In *Words of Wm. Booth* compiled by Cyril Barnes we are reminded of this passion especially when it came to the time for decision in the prayer meeting:

Whenever Wm. Booth preached he developed his thoughts toward the moment when he would appeal to his listeners to make a decision to serve Christ—on the spot. He would call them to come forward and kneel at the penitent-form and then launch into a prayer meeting.

In his earlier days he led this part of the meeting himself, but by 1890 he was beginning to feel the strain of taking full charge of protracted gatherings and needed help.

He was conducting a campaign in Durham. Assistance was essential, so he 'wired' Colonel John Lawley to come at once. He could sing; he had outstanding earnestness. Surely he he would be the ideal leader of the General's prayer meetings!

Lawley passed the test, and for 22 years the two men worked together. Lawley would carefully select the choruses to be used and make sure that the tunes were also helpful. In prayer meetings Wm. Booth would pray—and watch—as Lawley appealed to sinners to seek the Saviour. The Spirit of God would be at work upon the congregation; a man would move toward the front. "Sing it again, Lawley!" the General would call. He was never happy unless there were seekers in his prayer meetings.

While it is understood that the issues of life are often resolved in private, much of Army preaching is directed toward decisions made at the penitent-form. In the preceding chapters the Founder has suggested steps that will help the officer to lead people to the point of decision.

The main ideas from *How to Preach* have been excerpted, some portions reworded, and put into summary form as follows:

1. The preacher must know in his own soul that the things he proclaims to others are what he declares them to be. There can be no effective

preaching of salvation without the actual personal experience of the things spoken of in the heart and mind of the speaker.

2. To speak effectively, the *aim* of an officer must be right; that is to say, he must be seeking to bring men and women to God and to make them act in harmony with their own welfare, and the Divine will.

3. The soul of an officer should be on fire and his whole energy engrossed with the importance of his subject.

4. Without earnestness preaching cannot be said to be worthy of the name, and must inevitably fail in gaining its end. That end is the conquest of the heart and as only the heart can speak with authority to the heart, it follows that unless the heart is in the talk it would be better not to talk at all.

5. There is a preparation beyond any mere gathering together of ideas. In order to speak effectively of the things of the Kingdom, the soul of the speaker must be wide awake to their importance, and to the responsibility of the opportunity presented at the moment when he endeavors to speak on them. The duty of dealing with men about their souls and the great realities of the eternal world is so immensely important, that every officer ought to come up to it with every faculty sensitive and active to the fullest extent.

6. The inward perception he attains of Divine things, the sight of Calvary and the Judgment Day, and of heaven and hell, the blessedness of salvation, and the terribleness of damnation, all tend together to stir his whole being.

7. Immediate action is the goal. You must always keep this in view. This purpose alone will determine the difference between you and ordinary sermonizers. They are content with a discourse that explains some doctrine, or sets forth some duty, or illustrates some piece of biblical history, or something else of the same kind. Not so you: your aim is to bring the very rebels against God who sit before you to His feet there and then—to make those who have already submitted themselves to His control better and happier and holier and more useful—and you want them to decide in favor of these things during that service.

8. He should always keep three things in view in all his preparation for the platform:
   a. He, himself, should be careful to understand what he is going to say to other people. If he doesn't, how can he expect other people to understand him? He should think, and pray and read his Bible, until all is plain to his own mind, and then he will be likely to make it plain to others.
   b. He should illustrate plentifully.
   c. As he goes along he should apply every-

thing to the hearts and conscience of his hearers. He must drive home the truth or it will be useless.

9. The speaker must be natural in the way he talks. He should struggle to forget even himself, that is, to lose himself in the discharge of his duty. While his is thinking about himself, or rather of what the people may think, or of what he is going to say next, or about anything but the salvation of the people, he will be hindered, if not actually disqualified, for his duty. The preacher must throw himself into the fight regardless of anything and everything. He should never mind what sort of a spectacle he makes. If he will give himself up to the task of securing victory, he will be very likely to gain it.

10. It is important for the preacher to speak up— make everybody hear him. When he stands up to speak, he should always remember that his business is to convey some particular ideas to the minds and hearts of the people, with a view to their being influenced thereby. But what he says will be of no service unless it can be heard, and that readily.

11. The preacher must make himself understood when he is heard. As he cannot benefit the hearers by anything he says unless they hear his words, even so his words will be of no service unless the hearers know their meaning, or grasp the ideas that he convey to them.

In George Scott Railton's pamphlet *The Pigeon Shop*
one sees the sincerity, the earnestness, the holy
desire of William Booth to let nothing interfere with
his responsibility to declare the message of God. The
Pigeon Shop was one of the first Christian Mission
posts. Located in a district known as Bethnal Green,
the Pigeon Shop was full from floor to ceiling of
pigeons in cages. Back of the shop was a room where
a handful of Christian Mission members came every
night to minister to whatever congregation turned up.
William Booth came one morning to this place to
find the room full of people, poorly clad and shivering.
The question crossed Railton's mind, what will William
Booth say to this gathering of human misery? That
God would find them housing, jobs, food, money,
respectability, human dignity? No, he could not tell
them that. He told them in very simple words that
God knew them, that He shared their misery, that
He loved them and had come to find them, just where
they were. What depths of human insight he showed,
what rare and sensitive knowledge of the human heart.

He stood before them, tall and young, with that
rare look of infinite tenderness and love which, we
are told, crossed his face when deeply moved, and
announced that he was to speak on the text "The
King's Daughter Is All Glorious Within!"

And there in that wretched room the eternal miracle
of Christ's redeeming grace took place in human hearts.
Men and women who scarcely knew what they asked,
walked out knowing that all things had become new.

From this unpromising situation went out redeemed men and women, but mostly women, "King's daughters, clothed in grace."

Thus in this incident recorded by Railton the Founder is seen putting into practice all of the suggestions he penned to his officers in his series of articles written in 1893.

O God of Pentecostal fame,
Can I not have that living flame
Burning where'er I go?
From sin and self and shame set free,
Can I not lead lost souls to Thee
And conquer every foe?

. . . William Booth

Part II

EXCERPTS FROM SERMONS OF WILLIAM BOOTH

THIS section consists of excerpts from *The Founder Speaks Again*, a book of William Booth's writings, chosen and arranged by Cyril J. Barnes and published in 1960. These articles and sermons reflect the Founder's insights into the heart and soul of Salvationist preaching. They are persuasive, inspiring, and as useful and thought-provoking today as when conceived and written by William Booth.

From Part I, Chapter 8 of *The Founder Speaks Again* (page 38):

. . . Now the real object for which The Salvation Army exists is known to us all. It is to save men; not merely civilize them.

The object is to save men from sin and hell, to bring them to God and to bring God to them; to build up the Kingdom of Heaven upon earth. The end of the Salvation Army officer is to convert men, to change their hearts and lives . . .

From Chapter 6 of *The Founder Speaks Again* (page 38):

There are a great many people on earth, and a growing number in Heaven, who have been converted through some personal word spoken by the lovers of Jesus at unexpected times and in unusual places.

The opportunities for this kind of usefulness are so numerous that they cannot be counted. They come to us every day, and to most of us many times a day. But alas! how often they come and go unnoted and unimproved! This should not be. I want to ask you to take advantage of them.

I want you to feel that if you wear our blessed uniform, or in any other way signify that you belong to the Army, people expect you to say something to them about eternal things.

In many cases your neglect of what appears to be a duty may cause some surprise, and even lead those who witness it to set you down as insincere, or as only half believing the great truths on which the Army lays so great a stress.

Of course, opportunities will ever be occurring to you to speak to the members of your own family about their spiritual interests. But it is not those opportunities to which, at this moment, I refer, important as they may be. Neither am I asking you to avail yourselves of every chance of speaking to your comrades on these subjects. I am asking for something more than this. I am urging you to seize every opportunity of putting in your word for salvation with the ungodly people around you.

I am not asking you to visit them in their homes, on their sick beds, in the drinking saloons, in the workshops or elsewhere, although that is important—very important—and multitudes of your comrades all over the world have been successful in such efforts. But I am asking you to drop a word or have a little conversation with the people you meet in the train or on the tram; that when you buy or sell, when you are at the mill, when you meet friends or strangers by the way, you should be ready to speak a word for God and salvation.

Now some of you will say, 'I cannot do that sort of thing. I never could. I do not like it.' Perhaps not. But just wait a bit. I shall hope to show you not only that you can do this kind of work, but how you may find pleasure in doing it.

In order to do this, I recommend you to make up your mind to speak about God's will to the first stranger that crosses your path after reading this message. Do not think it absolutely necessary to decide beforehand what you shall say. The Holy Spirit will supply you with words, and bless you in speaking . . .

In speaking to strangers, be careful not to give needless offence. Speak kindly and gently and with all due courtesy and respect, and you will be surprised how far you can go without creating ill feeling . . .

Be sure and deal faithfully when you do speak. In many cases you can create interest by relating something of your own experience. Testimony is a wonderful thing and, when given modestly, with faith in God, generally moves the hearts of those who hear it . . .

Do not be discouraged if your words are rejected, or received with scorn, or even cast back in your teeth with sneers or curses. You can remember that this was the experience of your Lord, and that it is no proof that you have not said the right thing and that it may not have the desired effect.

It is not you who do the work, but the truth you speak. Unknown to you, the leaven you have imparted may be working in the heart you have approached and the seed you have sown may be destined to bring forth precious fruit.

From Part IV, Chapter 8 of *The Founder Speaks Again* (page 167):

Sixty-five years ago I chose the salvation of men and the extension of the Kingdom of Jesus Christ as the supreme object for which I would live and labor.

Although that choice was made in my early youth, in much ignorance of the world and of the religious needs of those about me, still it was not arrived at without much thought and some information; and that purpose is still, and will be to the end, the object which has shaped and mastered the thoughts, ambitions and activities of my whole life.

From the hour of my first prayer meetings in one of the cottage homes of my native town, down to the present moment, that object has been the governing principle of my life. The adornment and flowers and music and other pleasant things connected with religious service have all been secondary to efficiency in the search for that object and success in attaining it.

My hourly usage with regard to every effort I put forth has been to ask myself: "What does this action contemplate? What will it achieve? Can it be improved upon?" I believe I can say that every conversation and prayer and song and address and meeting I have had a hand in, has been valued in proportion to its ability to promote the realization of that great purpose . . . .

The interest awakened in my soul by the object on which, at the beginning, my heart was set, led me to study carefully the lives and conduct of those servants of God around me who had achieved any remarkable success in religious warfare, and from whom I might hope to learn something bearing on the work before me.

Then I have hunted the world over to find successful soul-winners, studying their histories and utterances, and striving to discover the principles and methods that led to their success. To many of them, now gone to their reward, I owe a deep debt of gratitude for the influence they exerted upon my career.

I think I can say that from the day of my conversion to God I have never read a biography, heard an address, or attended a meeting, without asking myself the question: 'Is there anything here from which I can learn how better to fulfill my own mission in enforcing the claims of my Lord; and saving the souls of men?'

All this has been of untold service in helping me

to store my mind, to mould my character, to kindle my spirit and to determine the nature of my warfare.

Those who have known me best and watched me most closely will largely attribute the success that God has been pleased to give me in dealing with the hearts and consciences of men to the fact that I am a man of feeling.

While accustomed to reason about every doctrine taught, every principle adopted and every method employed, I cannot afford to neglect emotion. Knowing the power for good that feeling exerts upon the people, and the benefits following its lawful use, I have ever felt myself all but powerless without its cooperation.

Indeed, my whole religious career has been characterized, and in some measure rendered effective, by this cooperation. The prayers I have offered, the faith I have exercised, the songs I have sung, the addresses I have delivered have, when anything like satisfactory to myself, been saturated with feeling, in fact their value has often been just in proportion to their ability to arouse feeling in my own heart, and in the hearts of those whom I have been trying to benefit.

This feeling has, no doubt, been in large measure the result of realization. Perhaps realization is only another word for feeling, for what is realization but the consciousness—that is, *the inward knowing* that things are what they appear? As some have heard me say: 'How can a man realize the existence of God, the forgiveness of sins, the value of his soul, the terrors of the Judgment Day, the glories of Heaven and the anguish of Hell without the feelings that correspond with those tremendous truths?' When truths are known to be what they seem, the heart will be stirred, and feeling must be the inevitable result.

From Part V, Chapter 4 of *The Founder Speaks Again* (page 194):

Some people are always complaining. Nothing is right with them. The weather is wrong, trade is wrong, their employers are wrong, their family is wrong—everything is wrong about them. If you belong to this class, can we find out the reason? Instead of the trade and the family and the neighbors and other people and things that you complain of so much as being wrong, perhaps after all it is yourself.

It is true that sinners' hearts are very hard, and that is the reason they are not converted; and some of your comrades are cold, and that is the reason why you don't get better meetings; and your officers may not be so clever and devoted as they might be, and that is the reason why you don't get more sinners into the barracks, and therefore things are not so bright and prosperous at your corps as they might be. But is there not another reason, which you have not mentioned, for your discomfort and the want of success in your corps, namely, that you are not right yourself? May there not be something terribly wanting in your own personal religion? Let me talk to you a little about it. Deal faithfully with your own soul. Tell the truth about your own heart to your own self, as fully as you would of anybody else's.

My first question is, Are you satisfied with your own religion? Other people can only make guesses about you. No matter how frequently they may be with you, they can still only infer what you really are from what you do. When people talk to you about your soul, about your state from the platform, or in the holiness meeting, you can put them off, tell them that you are right. I have no doubt you hope you will be when death or judgment finds you. Tell the truth now. Are you really and truly satisfied with your state? Can you look up to God and say, 'The effect produced on me and in me by my Father's love and my Saviour's sacrifice, and the operations of the Holy Ghost and the teachings of the Bible and the labors of my comrades and the wonderful opportunities that I enjoy, is such that it gives me satisfaction'?

More particularly:

1. Are you satisfied with what you realize of God in your own heart? You know the teachings of the Bible, and the experience of holy men and women justify us in expecting that God will talk to our hearts, tell of the forgiveness of sins, commune with us by the way, comfort us in sorrow and satisfy us with the revelation of His love. Are you satisified with what you have and what God reveals to you?

2. Are you satisfied with what you personally know of the cleansing Blood of Jesus Christ? You believe that that Blood was shed to remove the memory

and the power and the impurity of sin. Are you satisfied with its effects upon your own heart? Does the Holy Ghost witness with your soul as distinctly as you believe He is willing to do, that the end of Christ's sufferings and death has been answered in you? Have you the measure of holiness which means deliverance from sin, which you believe is your privilege? As you look in upon your heart, are you satisfied that you have reached just the condition which God wants you to reach, and therefore which pleases Him, and He looks down upon you from Heaven?

3. Are you satisfied with the way in which you discharge the duties of life as a husband, wife, father, mother, brother, sister, son, daughter, master, servant —as the case may be? Out of these relationships in which you stand to those about you numerous duties arise; when you look them over, are you satisfied with the way in which you discharge them?

4. Are you satisfied with what you are doing for the salvation of the world? You believe that people who live in sin—in the daily and hourly transgression of the commandments of God—are in danger every moment of the damnation of Hell. You say so in your speeches and songs and prayers and conversation. You say so in the religion you profess. The Bible, which claims to be the word of God, and in which you believe, says so most plainly.

Now this belief demands that you should act according to it. Do you? Nay, is your action such as gives you satisfaction? When you think of the poor people who are damned already; who have gone to Hell from your own doors, or your own neighborhood, are you satisfied? Can you rest feeling satisfied that you did what you could for them? When you go to bed at night and think of the thousands around you who will go to sleep on the brink of the bottomless pit, are you satisfied that you have done during that day what you could to wake them up? When you think how Jesus Christ's love and sacrifice are despised, do you get rest by thinking that you are doing what you can with your time and money and family and ability to bring the foul rebellion of the devil to an end, and bring the rebellious world to His feet?

Is it as well with you as it was when you were first converted? Doubtless you know a great deal more than you did then; can sing better, pray more fluently and talk far more cleverly; know a great deal more of your Bible, and have learnt all about the plans and reasons and methods of The Salvation Army. You are better off in your circumstances, more respected by your neighbors, have acquired a large circle of Salvationist friends who love you and think you a blessed holy saint. But are you satisfied in your own heart that your love for God and your devotion to the salvation of men is equal to what it was the week after you were converted? Nay, are you satisfied that it is what it ought to be? I don't ask you, Is God satisfied or the angels satisfied, or the corps satisfied, with your religion—but are you satisfied yourself?

If not, you know the remedy. Go down before God,

repent, confess, consecrate, believe, be filled and go forth to conquer.

Additonal suggestions for messages from the Founder:

The Founder Speaks Again; A Selection of the Writings of William Booth, chosen and arranged by Cyril J. Barnes. London, Salvationist Publishing and Supplies, 1960. 204 p., photographs.

> *The Last Public Address* (p. 169)
>> Delivered in the Royal Albert Hall, London—May 9, 1912
>
> *The Spirit of Life* (p. 35)
>> International Congress Address—1904 (Field Officers' Councils)

The General's Letters, 1885. Being a Reprint from "The War Cry" of Letters to Soldiers and Friends Scattered Throughout the World. London, International Headquarters, 1889. 204 p., illus.

> *Gifts of the Spirit* (p. 82)
>> From *The War Cry*—March 14, 1885

Salvation Soldiery; a series of Addresses on the Requirements of Jesus Christ's Service, by the Founder of The Salvation Army. 1st ed. London, Salvationist Publishing and Supplies, n.d. 138 p.

> *Our New Name—The Salvationist* (p. 11)
> *Holiness* (p. 72)

You must have a new energy.
What is the reproach of religion?
That there is no heart in it. The in-
fidels say so; the politicians say so;
business men say so; theatrical
people say so. In fact everybody
knows that there is enthusiasm in
politics, enthusiasm in business, en-
thusiasm in pleasure, enthusiasm in
war, and in everything else except
that which calls more loudly for it
than them all—the following of the
Crucified to the Conquest of the
World . . .

. . . William Booth

Part III

WHAT OTHERS SAY

In the selected writings of the preceding chapters, the Founder chose to emphasize certain points as being important for a preacher of the Word to know and use, if he is to be effective and to discharge his responsibility faithfully. The conviction that there is no work in the world that can be compared with that of preaching the gospel—standing in Christ's stead—teaching and persuading men to be reconciled to God, was demonstrated by William Booth's life of dedicated and inspired preaching.

After retirement General Albert Orsborn wrote "The import and the urgency of the gospel message have burned me up, and carried me on. Only in my first year or two did I think I knew how to preach the saving truth of God in Christ. For at least 45 years I have prayed and struggled to know better and to fulfil better what Paul called 'this ministry.' Never satisfied, but always thankful for the privilege of our sacred Army platform, I have often exclaimed—'I cannot tell it!

I cannot tell it! It is too much for me—this gospel of reconciliation—and I shall die with my message in me, still undelivered" *(The Officer*-May, June 1954).

Thus said the sixth General of The Salvation Army. It underlines thoughts expressed by the first General, the Founder of The Salvation Army. He was caught up with the importance of the gospel message and the necessity to deliver it in the most effective way possible—a way that would result in souls seeking the Saviour. Few of us have heard the Founder preach, but we do have comments and observations by those who lived in his day and heard him preach. What are their observations? Is he an example of the kind of preaching he has outlined and recommended in the preceding pages?

An examination of *Chapter I* reveals that the key word for the Founder's preaching was "earnestness." He taught that preaching is not to be a performance, an act, but that the preacher must be in earnest as he expounds from the Word. One should preach with *discernment,* with *feeling* for *results.*

Now let's take a look at what William Booth said about himself, as recorded in Cyril Barnes' *Words of William Booth* (pages 71, 72). The Founder had received an invitation from Buckingham Palace to meet King Edward VII on June 24, 1904. The interview was of a most gracious and cordial nature. The General was delighted to be able to speak of the work of his people in 49 countries. The King complimented him and asked how the churches viewed his work. "Sir," replied the 75 year old warrior "they imitate me." The King was amused and requested him to write in his autograph album. William Booth wrote:

> Some men's ambition is art.
> Some men's ambition is fame.
> Some men's ambition is gold.
> My ambition is the souls of men.

In those words William Booth summed up his life's work.

His son, Bramwell Booth, writes in *Echoes and Memories* (pages 7,8):

> I touch with hesitation the subject of my father's religion. How, indeed, can it be dealt with in a page of reminiscence! But at least, this may be said: that it was never a platform pose. The religion he commended to his fellows with such directness and sincerity was the religion which he himself accepted with all his heart and lived with all his might.
>
> His illustrations were innumerable, but they were not mere attachments to his addresses. They were woven into the texture so that it became almost impossible to recall the illustration without remembering the truth which it had been chosen to enforce. The illustration itself, without any subsequent embroidery, conveyed its lesson. The same was often true of his texts, for though his texts were frequently no more than doorways through which

he entered upon some great principle or truth, he saw to it that they were deeply set in the minds of his hearers. I shall never forget the effect upon great audiences of the repetition of texts such as *"This year thou shalt die;" "The great day of His wrath is come, who shall be able to stand;" "Serve the Lord with gladness;" "Be sure your sins will find you out;" "Blessed are the pure in heart;" "And the flood came, and took them all away."*

The Founder makes it clear, as recorded in *Chapter II,* that the single aim of preaching should be "God and souls." This begins with preparation. The preacher does not wait until he has arrived on the platform. Right from the beginning the first thought must be "souls." The sermon should be prepared with the thought that under the power of the Holy Spirit conviction will come to the sinner and he will respond. Preparation thus relates not only to the sermon but the preacher himself. Paul tells us in First Corinthians 1:21, *"For after that in the wisdom of God the world by wisdom knew not God, it pleased God by the foolishness of preaching to save them that believe."*

Bramwell Booth in *Echoes and Memories* (page 24), writes "It is the preaching of Jesus Christ and His Salvation, with a direct and arresting message, that he will be most remembered in all the lands he visited. His preaching was barbed. Its purpose was not merely to instruct or edify, still less to tickle the ears, but to bring men to decision on the most momentous questions which can engage the human mind. Its aim was as definite as the speech of a counsel to a jury. His earnestness, his deep yearning for souls, his profound sympathy with sinners, were always uppermost and lowermost. What he said was so obviously a part of himself that he disarmed his critics, who then and there began to believe in him; until they responded to his message."

Sallie Chesham in *Born to Battle* (page 31), points out that there were results—souls at the altar. William Booth was a man on fire for the souls of men.

> . . . William conducted revivals with amazing success. In four months 1,739 people sought salvation at nine separate centers. There was a realism about him that gripped his hearers. Perhaps they sensed that evil was as apparent to him as good, damnation as close as heaven. He talked as if he believed not only in a just and good God but also in a personal devil. The person of Jesus Christ was more important than the "package" of any creed. He talked and acted like a man who, mortally beset by evil, had overcome the aggressor through Divine power. His listeners, largely drawn from the middle classes, sometimes objected to his forthrightness, his imagery, his persistent presentation of self-willed men born in sin, but they could not withstand his power. He appeared then, as throughout his life, as one having authority. He rarely sought

to prove Christianity, and his preaching was
not an examination of *what* to believe but in
whom to believe.

Chapter III refers to the Founder's statements on the
importance of having something to talk about. A
topic—a peg—related to a truth that will not only
impress the listener but as William Booth puts it "cling
to the minds and memories of the hearers." The
sermon should apply to the people and make them
think about their responsibility to God.

Daniel Poling, at one time editor of the *Christian
Herald,* said about his own experience *(Guideposts—*
March 1957):

"When I was ordained a Christian minister 50 years
ago, my preaching was based on three assumptions:

1. The men and women to whom I preached needed
   Jesus Christ.
2. Jesus Christ is always present to meet the needs
   of those to whom I spoke.
3. The least, and indeed, the most that I can do is
   to make it possible for the two to meet."

William Booth was a fine example of relating the
message of the gospel to the needs of the people.
Sallie Chesham in *Born to Battle* mentions this
(page 30):

His preaching stabbed the spirit, then offered
the healing of Divine love. He chose dramatic
and fighting subjects which urged his hearers
to stand against sin. He wrote Catherine
hurriedly for outlines—"I want a sermon on

the flood, one on Jonah, and one on the Judgment. Send some bare thoughts, some clear, startling outlines. Nothing moves people like the terrific. They must have hellfire flashed before their face or they will not move."

Bramwell Booth, in *Echoes and Memories* (pages 22 and 23), describes the Founder's concern in reaching his listeners with basic truths using direct language. He writes:

William Booth's subjects were nearly always heart subjects. Some of his critics have denied him the philosophic mind, and others have found fault with the lack of scientific range in his preaching, but his great work could never have been done along that line. He did not neglect reason in his audiences, but reasoned with them of sin, and of righteousness, and of judgment—always of judgment—and the evil heart of rebellion and unbelief in them was ever before him. He was a messenger to the heart of mankind—a courier taking the most direct route, and making all possible haste. His vocabulary was the vocabulary of the common people. Clear, direct, vigorous, simple. He scarcely used an expression which would puzzle the most ignorant.

Chapter IV refers to the preaching itself—the delivery of the message. William Booth underlines the importance of:

> being yourself,
> speaking clearly,
> speaking to the audience,
> speaking to be heard.

This is the practical, everyday aspect of peaching. We need to say it again and again. The preacher makes the message. Preaching is not the performance of an hour. It is the outflow of a life. Paul termed it "my gospel." The gospel had been entrusted to Paul, experienced by him and exclaimed by him. It has been said, "no candle on the altar of a church will ever substitute for a flame in the heart of a preacher in the pulpit."

The Founder's son, Bramwell Booth, in *Echoes and Memories* (pages 18, 19, 22) aptly illustrates William Booth's ability to exemplify his admonitions as stated above.

> His appearance did help him to obtain attention. His splendid head and fine profile and keen, flashing eyes, his outstretched arms, his scarlet jersey, his erect and yet supple figure, swayed at times like a tree in the wind, all gave the most casual listener the impression of something quiet out of the ordinary . . . They put an audience in an expectant mood. His voice was powerful without being loud. It was a voice that wore well. On occasion when he spoke in such places as the Albert Hall, or in Madison Square Garden in New York, or the Circus Busch in Berlin he could

by an effort compass an immense area and hold a great throng spellbound. These were, of course, the days before amplifiers.

Cyril Barnes, writing about the Founder in *Words of William Booth* (page 68), sums up Chapter IV's suggestions for effectively delivering the message in the following description and quote:

Mr. Booth employed very simple language in his comments . . . frequently repeating the same sentence several times as if he was afraid his hearers would forget . . . not a word was uttered by him that could be misconstrued; not a doctrine was propounded that was beyond the comprehension of those to whom it was addressed . . . When counselling his officers on the art of public speaking, he would say: "Use words that Mary Ann (a servant) will understand, and you will be sure to make yourself plain to her mistress; whereas if you speak only to her mistress, you will very likely miss her, and Mary Ann as well."

William Booth is considered to be one of the most successful platform speakers of his, or any other, time. Quite obviously he practiced the methods advocated in his articles on the subject in "The Officer" magazine—and they worked. They will work for you also. Remember your audiences of "Mary Anns," and the importance of presenting to them, clearly and plainly, the message of God's Holy Word.

The value of the Bible as a book lies not in the words employed but in ideas conveyed by those words. Those words must therefore be the most desirable which convey the meaning of the inspired writers to those to whom they may now be addressed. For this reason I should very much like to see a Bible rendered into the English language as now spoken by English-speaking people throughout the world. It seems to me however that the only translation, that in the long run will be of any value is the reproduction of the Scriptures in the lives of men and women; that makes their worth.

. . . William Booth

CHARLES TALMADGE

CHARLES Talmadge devoted many of his 44 years as a Salvation Army officer to the training of cadets for officership. In his early years, soon after his commissioning in 1932, he served on the staff of the School for Officers' Training in New York City.

After assignments including posts as corps officer in the greater New York area, director of youth programs in eastern Pennsylvania and New England, and divisional secretary in northeastern Ohio, Colonel Talmadge returned to the New York School for Officers' Training where he held various appointments over the next ten years. He was assistant training principal from 1962 to 1964 and, in this capacity, he was responsible for instituting a new method for training married cadets.

While a student at New York University, Colonel Talmadge was awarded a scholarship to study in Jerusalem during the summer of 1959. He received his degree from New York University's School for Education in 1961.

Later in the sixties Colonel Talmadge was the principal of the School for Officers' Training in Atlanta, Georgia, and of the eastern territory's school in Suffern, New York.

Colonel Talmadge retired in 1976, making his home in Atlanta where he had spent his last two years as secretary for personnel at the territorial headquarters.

Charles Talmadge's early commitment to God's service carries over to his retirement years. Much in demand as a guest speaker, he continues to gain wide recognition for his effective public ministry.

New York, N.Y.—3/79